Contents

General Knowledge

1) West Brom lost their first game of the 21st century 2-0 to which team on the 3rd of January 2000?

2) Which company was the club's main shirt sponsor during the 2004/05 Premier League season?

3) Who was West Brom's top scorer during the 2006/07 Championship campaign with 20 goals?

4) Saido Berahino made his debut in a League Cup match against which side in August 2012?

5) Who scored the winner for Derby County in the 2007 Championship Play Off Final?

6) Who became the first South Korean to play for the Baggies after signing in December 2007?

7) Who made his debut for the club against Wigan in a 3-2 defeat in the Premier League aged 16 years and 3 months old in May 2013?

8) Which goalkeeper appeared aged 39 years and 6 months old against Middlesbrough in April 2010?

9) What squad number did Oliver Burke wear during his time at West Brom?

10) Who captained the team on his debut against Burnley in February 2015?

11) Who scored an embarrassing own goal to start the scoring in the 5-0 home loss to Leeds in December 2020?

12) Ben Foster saved a penalty from which player in the 2-0 win at Anfield in February 2013?

13) Who scored a hat-trick on the final day of the season to claim a 3-3 draw at Newcastle in 2011?

14) In which year did Jeremy Peace sell the club to Chinese investment group Lai Guochuan?

15) West Brom finished second to claim automatic promotion from Division One in 2002, but which team finished just behind them in third?

16) How many points did the Baggies win in the Premier League during the 2020/21 season as they were relegated back to the Championship?

17) Who won the BBC Goal of the Month award for his strike against Spurs in April 2011?

18) Which side knocked West Brom out of the Division One Play Offs at the Semi Final stage in 2001?

19) The club enjoyed a run in the Premier League from 2010-2018, but what was their highest league finish in that time?

20) Chris Brunt made his final Baggies appearance against which team in 2020?

Transfers Part One

1) Who was sold to Juventus in January 2000?

2) Jason Roberts was purchased from which club in the summer of 2000?

3) Which defender moved from West Brom to Cardiff in September 2000?

4) Which goalkeeper arrived from Portsmouth in January 2001?

5) From which side was Danny Dichio bought in November 2001?

6) Who joined on a free from Manchester United in July 2002?

7) Martin Albrechtsen signed from which European club in 2004?

8) Who was brought in from Ferencvaros in July 2004?

9) Which forward was sold to Leeds in May 2005?

10) Curtis Davies arrived from which club in the summer of 2005?

11) Who moved from West Brom to Norwich City in the 2006 January transfer window?

12) From which team was Kevin Phillips purchased in August 2006?

13) Who was brought in from Hibernian in July 2007?

14) Who did the Baggies sign from Sheffield Wednesday in August 2007?

15) Which player moved to Sheffield Wednesday on a free in the summer of 2007?

16) Marek Cech was bought from which team in July 2008?

17) Simon Cox came in from which side in July 2009?

18) Craig Beattie moved from West Brom to which club in 2009?

19) Which player did West Brom sign from RB Salzburg in August 2010?

20) Who joined on a free from Ipswich Town in May 2011?

Cup Games

1) Which non-league team did West Brom beat 7-0 in the FA Cup Third Round in January 2015?

2) Who scored a hat-trick in the 5-1 win at Bristol Rovers in the FA Cup Quarter Final in 2008?

3) Which club knocked the Baggies out of the FA Cup in both 2010 and 2011?

4) Who scored deep into stoppage time to force a replay with Chesterfield in the FA Cup Third Round in 2023?

5) Arsenal beat West Brom by what score in the League Cup Second Round in August 2021?

6) Who scored the winner for Portsmouth in the 2008 FA Cup Semi Final?

7) West Brom set up a League Cup Quarter Final with Arsenal in December 2003 by beating which side 2-0 in the previous round?

8) Who was in goal as Peterborough were beaten on penalties in the FA Cup Fourth Round in February 2016?

9) Which three players scored in the 3-0 FA Cup Fourth Round win at Wolves in January 2007?

10) By what score did West Brom lose to Stoke in the League Cup First Round in August 2023?

Starting Elevens

Name the starting team for the following games from the initials given

The 5-1 win over Wolves at Molineux in February 2012

BF
GM
JO
SR
PS
LR
JM
YM
JT
MAF
PO

Starting Elevens (2)

The 1-0 loss to Manchester United in West Brom's first ever Premiership game in August 2002

RH

LS

PG

DM

NC

SG

IB

AJ

DM

DD

JR

Starting Elevens (3)

The dramatic 2-0 win over Portsmouth to claim Premier League survival on the last day of the 2004/05 season

TK
MA
KR
PR
NC
TG
ZG
JG
RW
KC
RE

Starting Elevens (4)

The final day 2-2 draw with QPR in July 2020 as the club claimed promotion back to the Premier League

SJ
KB
SA
DO
DF
FK
RS
JL
CR
GD
MP

Starting Elevens (5)

The 2-0 win over QPR in May 2008 that secured the Championship title on the last day of the campaign

DK
LB
CH
PR
NC
CB
ZG
JG
RK
RB
KP

Memorable Games

1) Peter Odemwingie scored a hat-trick in the 5-1 demolition of Wolves in February 2012, but which other two players scored for the Baggies that day?

2) In which year did West Brom draw 5-5 with Manchester United in Alex Ferguson's last game in management?

3) Who scored the only goal in the 1-0 win at Old Trafford in the Premier League in April 2018?

4) Which team did West Brom hammer 7-0 at home in the Championship in May 2007?

5) Who scored the last minute winner against Bradford in April 2002 to put West Brom within touching distance of Premiership promotion?

6) Who was the Liverpool manager during the 3-0 opening day win for West Brom in August 2012?

7) West Brom claimed their first ever Premiership win by beating which team 1-0 at home in August 2002?

8) Who scored the only goal in the 1-0 win at Villa Park in the Premier League in September 2015?

9) QPR were beaten by what score line at The Hawthorns in August 2018?

10) Kevin Phillips scored in stoppage time to claim a 1-0 win over which team in the Championship in March 2008?

Red Cards

1) Who was sent off in West Brom's first ever Premiership match, the 1-0 defeat at Manchester United in August 2002?

2) Which two players were sent off in the 2-1 defeat at Blackpool in November 2010?

3) Claudio Yacob was given a straight red during a 2-0 defeat to which team in November 2014?

4) West Brom beat which team 1-0 away from home in the Premiership in January 2006 despite Darren Moore receiving two yellows in the first half?

5) Youssouf Mulumbu was comically sent off for kicking the ball at which West Ham player in March 2013?

6) James McClean and Salomon Rondon were both given their marching orders in the 2-1 defeat to which side in 2015?

7) Who was sent off in the loss to Sheffield United in Steve Bruce's first match in charge?

8) Which player was given a red card after a VAR review during the loss to Crystal Palace in December 2020?

9) Jay Rodriguez had his red card rescinded after being dismissed against which team in December 2018?

10) Gareth McAuley was sent off against Manchester City in a case of mistaken identity in March 2015, the red card was later correctly transferred to which of his team mates?

Anagrams

*Identify the players from the anagrams
and the years they represented the club*

1) *Lustrous Hell*
   2001-2007

2) *Worn Lion Walker*
   2002-2008

3) *Claw Hip Orchard*
   2005-2008

4) *Hot Shorn Jan*
   2006-2008

5) *Hairnets Molts*
   2007-2010

6) *Rap Launchers*
   2010-2012

7) *Baker Rugs Mourns*
   2012-2014

8) *Disarranged Laden*
   2015-2016

9) *Risking Babe*
   2017-2021

10) *Bad Divot Nut*
    2020-2023

Managers

1) Who was the West Brom manager at the beginning of the 21st century?

2) After Bryan Robson left in 2006, who took caretaker charge for the next four games (of which he won three and drew one)?

3) Tony Mowbray beat which team 3-0 in his first game in charge in October 2006?

4) Who did Roy Hodgson replace as gaffer in February 2011?

5) How many of his 17 matches in charge did Pepe Mel win?

6) West Brom lost at home to Chelsea in Tony Pulis' last game in the hot seat, but what was the final score?

7) Which team was Alan Pardew managing in his previous job before taking over at the Baggies?

8) Who oversaw the team as caretaker after Darren Moore left in March 2019?

9) Who did West Brom lose 3-0 at home to in Sam Allardyce's first game as manager?

10) Who replaced Allardyce as permanent manager ahead of the 2021/22 campaign?

First Goals

Can you name the team that these players scored their first goal for the club against from the options below?

1) Scott Dobie
   Cambridge United
   Oxford United
   Exeter City

2) Danny Dichio
   Sunderland
   Middlesbrough
   Sheffield Wednesday

3) Robert Earnshaw
   Newcastle United
   Southampton
   Birmingham City

4) Nathan Ellington
   Wigan Athletic
   Bradford City
   Northampton Town

5) Kanu
   Fulham
   Portsmouth
   Leeds United

6) Chris Brunt
   Huddersfield Town
   Ipswich Town
   Scunthorpe

7) Romelu Lukaku
   Liverpool
   Chelsea
   Manchester United

8) Salomon Rondon
   Stoke City
   Leicester City
   Tottenham Hotspur

9) Karlan Grant
   Huddersfield Town
   Reading
   Brighton

10) Brandon Thomas-Asante
    Luton Town
    Burnley
    Wycombe Wanderers

Transfers Part Two

1) Billy Jones joined on a free transfer from which team in the summer of 2011?

2) Roman Bednar joined which team on a free in January 2012?

3) Who signed from Werder Bremen in August 2012?

4) Chris Wood was sold to which team in the 2013 January transfer window?

5) Who joined the club from PSG in August 2013?

6) Peter Odemwingie was sold to which club in 2013?

7) Which player joined on a free from Burnley in July 2014?

8) West Brom signed which two players from Manchester United in August 2015?

9) Joleon Lescott was sold to which team in September 2015?

10) Allan-Romeo Nyom was bought from where in 2016?

11) Which two players moved from West Brom to Stoke in the 2017 January transfer window?

12) Olivier Burke was brought in from which side in 2017?

13) Who signed from Scunthorpe in July 2018?

14) Wes Hoolahan signed for which team after leaving the Baggies in August 2019?

15) Who was bought from Wigan in September 2020?

16) Who made the switch from West Brom to LA Galaxy in January 2021?

17) Alex Mowatt was signed from which team in July 2021?

18) Matheus Pereira was sold to which club in August 2021?

19) Who signed from Crystal Palace in September 2022?

20) Josh Maja signed from which club ahead of the 2023/24 season?

Answers

General Knowledge Answers

1) West Brom lost their first game of the 21st century 2-0 to which team on the 3rd of January 2000?
Barnsley

2) Which company was the club's main shirt sponsor during the 2004/05 Premier League season?
T Mobile

3) Who was West Brom's top scorer during the 2006/07 Championship campaign with 20 goals?
Diomansy Kamara

4) Saido Berahino made his debut in a League Cup match against which side in August 2012?
Yeovil Town

5) Who scored the winner for Derby County in the 2007 Championship Play Off Final?
Stephen Pearson

6) Who became the first South Korean to play for the Baggies after signing in December 2007?
Do-heon Kim

7) Who made his debut for the club against Wigan in a 3-2 defeat in the Premier League aged 16 years and 3 months old in May 2013?
Izzy Brown

8) Which goalkeeper appeared aged 39 years and 6 months old against Middlesbrough in April 2010?
Dean Kiely

9) What squad number did Oliver Burke wear during his time at West Brom?
17

10) Who captained the team on his debut against Burnley in February 2015?
Darren Fletcher

11) Who scored an embarrassing own goal to start the scoring in the 5-0 home loss to Leeds in December 2020?
Romaine Sawyers

12) Ben Foster saved a penalty from which player in the 2-0 win at Anfield in February 2013?
Steven Gerrard

13) Who scored a hat-trick on the final day of the season to claim a 3-3 draw at Newcastle in 2011?
Somen Tchoyi

14) In which year did Jeremy Peace sell the club to Chinese investment group Lai Guochuan?
2016

15) West Brom finished second to claim automatic promotion from Division One in 2002, but which team finished just behind them in third?

Wolves

16) How many points did the Baggies win in the Premier League during the 2020/21 season as they were relegated back to the Championship?

26

17) Who won the BBC Goal of the Month award for his strike against Spurs in April 2011?

Simon Cox

18) Which side knocked West Brom out of the Division One Play Offs at the Semi Final stage in 2001?

Bolton

19) The club enjoyed a run in the Premier League from 2010-2018, but what was their highest league finish in that time?
Eighth

20) Chris Brunt made his final Baggies appearance against which team in 2020?
QPR

Transfers Part One Answers

1) Who was sold to Juventus in January 2000?
   Enzo Maresca

2) Jason Roberts was purchased from which club in the summer of 2000?
   Bristol Rovers

3) Which defender moved from West Brom to Cardiff in September 2000?
   Danny Gabbidon

4) Which goalkeeper arrived from Portsmouth in January 2001?
   Russell Hoult

5) From which side was Danny Dichio bought in November 2001?
   Sunderland

6) Who joined on a free from Manchester United in July 2002?
   Ronnie Wallwork

7) Martin Albrechtsen signed from which European club in 2004?
FC Copenhagen

8) Who was brought in from Ferencvaros in July 2004?
Zoltan Gera

9) Which forward was sold to Leeds in May 2005?
Rob Hulse

10) Curtis Davies arrived from which club in the summer of 2005?
Luton Town

11) Who moved from West Brom to Norwich City in the 2006 January transfer window?
Robert Earnshaw

12) From which team was Kevin Phillips purchased in August 2006?
Aston Villa

13) Who was brought in from Hibernian in July 2007?
Shelton Martis

14) Who did the Baggies sign from Sheffield Wednesday in August 2007?
Chris Brunt

15) Which player moved to Sheffield Wednesday on a free in the summer of 2007?
Steve Watson

16) Marek Cech was bought from which team in July 2008?
Porto

17) Simon Cox came in from which side in July 2009?
Swindon Town

18) Craig Beattie moved from West Brom to which club in 2009?
Swansea City

19) Which player did West Brom sign from RB Salzburg in August 2010?
Somen Tchoyi

20) Who joined on a free from Ipswich Town in May 2011?
Gareth McAuley

Cup Games Answers

1) Which non-league team did West Brom beat 7-0 in the FA Cup Third Round in January 2015?
Gateshead

2) Who scored a hat-trick in the 5-1 win at Bristol Rovers in the FA Cup Quarter Final in 2008?
Ishmael Miller

3) Which club knocked the Baggies out of the FA Cup in both 2010 and 2011?
Reading

4) Who scored deep into stoppage time to force a replay with Chesterfield in the FA Cup Third Round in 2023?
Brandon Thomas-Asante

5) Arsenal beat West Brom by what score in the League Cup Second Round in August 2021?
West Brom 0-6 Arsenal

6) Who scored the winner for Portsmouth in the 2008 FA Cup Semi Final?
Kanu

7) West Brom set up a League Cup Quarter Final with Arsenal in December 2003 by beating which side 2-0 in the previous round?
Manchester United

8) Who was in goal as Peterborough were beaten on penalties in the FA Cup Fourth Round in February 2016?
Ben Foster

9) Which three players scored in the 3-0 FA Cup Fourth Round win at Wolves in January 2007?
Diomansy Kamara, Kevin Phillips and Zoltan Gera

10) By what score did West Brom lose to Stoke in the League Cup First Round in August 2023?
Stoke 2-1 West Brom

Starting Elevens Answers

The 5-1 win over Wolves at Molineux in February 2012

Ben Foster
Gareth McAuley
Jonas Olsson
Steven Reid
Paul Scharner
Liam Ridgewell
James Morrison
Youssef Mulumbu
Jerome Thomas
Marc Antoine Fortune
Peter Odemwingie

Starting Elevens Answers (2)

The 1-0 loss to Manchester United in West Brom's first ever Premiership game in August 2002

Russell Hoult
Larus Sigurdsson
Phil Gilchrist
Darren Moore
Neil Clement
Sean Gregan
Igor Balis
Andy Johnson
Derek McInnes
Danny Dichio
Jason Roberts

Starting Elevens Answers (3)

The dramatic 2-0 win over Portsmouth to claim Premier League survival on the last day of the 2004/05 season

Tomasz Kuszczak
Martin Albrechtsen
Kieran Richardson
Paul Robinson
Neil Clement
Thomas Gaardsoe
Zoltan Gera
Jonathan Greening
Ronnie Wallwork
Kevin Campbell
Robert Earnshaw

Starting Elevens Answers (4)

The final day 2-2 draw with QPR in July 2020 as the club claimed promotion back to the Premier League

Sam Johnstone
Kyle Bartley
Semi Ajayi
Dara O'Shea
Darnell Furlong
Filip Krovinovic
Romaine Sawyers
Jake Livermore
Callum Robinson
Grady Diangana
Matheus Pereira

Starting Elevens Answers (5)

The 2-0 win over QPR in May 2008 that secured the Championship title on the last day of the campaign

Dean Kiely
Leon Barnett
Carl Hoefkens
Paul Robinson
Neil Clement
Chris Brunt
Zoltan Gera
Jonathan Greening
Robert Koren
Roman Bednar
Kevin Phillips

Memorable Games Answers

1) Peter Odemwingie scored a hat-trick in the 5-1 demolition of Wolves in February 2012, but which other two players scored for the Baggies that day?
Jonas Olsson and Keith Andrews

2) In which year did West Brom draw 5-5 with Manchester United in Alex Ferguson's last game in management?
2013

3) Who scored the only goal in the 1-0 win at Old Trafford in the Premier League in April 2018?
Jay Rodriguez

4) Which team did West Brom hammer 7-0 at home in the Championship in May 2007?
Barnsley

5) Who scored the last minute winner against Bradford in April 2002 to put West Brom within touching distance of Premiership promotion?
Igor Balis

6) Who was the Liverpool manager during the 3-0 opening day win for West Brom in August 2012?
Brendan Rogers

7) West Brom claimed their first ever Premiership win by beating which team 1-0 at home in August 2002?
Fulham

8) Who scored the only goal in the 1-0 win at Villa Park in the Premier League in September 2015?
Saido Berahino

9) QPR were beaten by what score line at The Hawthorns in August 2018?
West Brom 7-1 QPR

10) Kevin Phillips scored in stoppage time to claim a 1-0 win over which team in the Championship in March 2008?
Sheffield Wednesday

Red Cards Answers

1) Who was sent off in West Brom's first ever Premiership match, the 1-0 defeat at Manchester United in August 2002?
Derek McInnes

2) Which two players were sent off in the 2-1 defeat at Blackpool in November 2010?
Pablo Ibanez and Gonzalo Jara

3) Claudio Yacob was given a straight red during a 2-0 defeat to which team in November 2014?
Chelsea

4) West Brom beat which team 1-0 away from home in the Premiership in January 2006 despite Darren Moore receiving two yellows in the first half?
Wigan

5) Youssouf Mulumbu was comically sent off for kicking the ball at which West Ham player in March 2013?
Gary O'Neil

6) James McClean and Salomon Rondon were both given their marching orders in the 2-1 defeat to which side in 2015?
Bournemouth

7) Who was sent off in the loss to Sheffield United in Steve Bruce's first match in charge?
Jake Livermore

8) Which player was given a red card after a VAR review during the loss to Crystal Palace in December 2020?
Matheus Pereira

9) Jay Rodriguez had his red card rescinded after being dismissed against which team in December 2018?
Sheffield Wednesday

10) Gareth McAuley was sent off against Manchester City in a case of mistaken identity in March 2015, the red card was later correctly transferred to which of his team mates?
Craig Dawson

Anagrams Answers

1) *Lustrous Hell*
   2001-2007
   Russell Hoult

2) *Worn Lion Walker*
   2002-2008
   Ronnie Wallwork

3) *Claw Hip Orchard*
   2005-2008
   Richard Chaplow

4) *Hot Shorn Jan*
   2006-2008
   John Hartson

5) *Hairnets Molts*
   2007-2010
   Shelton Martis

6) *Rap Launchers*
2010-2012
Paul Scharner

7) *Baker Rugs Mourns*
2012-2014
Markus Rosenberg

8) *Disarranged Laden*
2015-2016
Anders Lindegaard

9) *Risking Babe*
2017-2021
Kieran Gibbs

10) *Bad Divot Nut*
2020-2023
David Button

Managers Answers

1) Who was the West Brom manager at the beginning of the 21st century?
Brian Little

2) After Bryan Robson left in 2006, who took caretaker charge for the next four games (of which he won three and drew one)?
Nigel Pearson

3) Tony Mowbray beat which team 3-0 in his first game in charge in October 2006?
Wolves

4) Who did Roy Hodgson replace as gaffer in February 2011?
Roberto Di Matteo

5) How many of his 17 matches in charge did Pepe Mel win?
Three

6) West Brom lost at home to Chelsea in Tony Pulis' last game in the hot seat, but what was the final score?
West Brom 0-7 Chelsea

7) Which team was Alan Pardew managing in his previous job before taking over at the Baggies?
Crystal Palace

8) Who oversaw the team as caretaker after Darren Moore left in March 2019?
James Shan

9) Who did West Brom lose 3-0 at home to in Sam Allardyce's first game as manager?
Aston Villa

10) Who replaced Allardyce as permanent manager ahead of the 2021/22 campaign?
Valerien Ismael

First Goals Answers

1) Scott Dobie
   Cambridge United

2) Danny Dichio
   Sheffield Wednesday

3) Robert Earnshaw
   Southampton

4) Nathan Ellington
   Bradford City

5) Kanu
   Fulham

6) Chris Brunt
   Scunthorpe

7) Romelu Lukaku
   Liverpool

8) Salomon Rondon
   Stoke City

9) Karlan Grant
   Brighton

10) Brandon Thomas-Asante
    Burnley

Transfers Part Two Answers

1) Billy Jones joined on a free transfer from which team in the summer of 2011?
Preston

2) Roman Bednar joined which team on a free in January 2012?
Blackpool

3) Who signed from Werder Bremen in August 2012?
Markus Rosenberg

4) Chris Wood was sold to which team in the 2013 January transfer window?
Leicester City

5) Who joined the club from PSG in August 2013?
Diego Lugano

6) Peter Odemwingie was sold to which club in 2013?
Cardiff City

7) Which player joined on a free from Burnley in July 2014?
Chris Baird

8) West Brom signed which two players from Manchester United in August 2015?
Jonny Evans and Anders Lindegaard

9) Joleon Lescott was sold to which team in September 2015?
Aston Villa

10) Allan-Romeo Nyom was bought from where in 2016?
Watford

11) Which two players moved from West Brom to Stoke in the 2017 January transfer window?
Saido Berahino and Darren Fletcher

12) Olivier Burke was brought in from which side in 2017?
RB Leipzig

13) Who signed from Scunthorpe in July 2018?
Conor Townsend

14) Wes Hoolahan signed for which team after leaving the Baggies in August 2019?
Newcastle Jets

15) Who was bought from Wigan in September 2020?
Cedric Kipre

16) Who made the switch from West Brom to LA Galaxy in January 2021?
Jonathan Bond

17) Alex Mowatt was signed from which team in July 2021?
Barnsley

18) Matheus Pereira was sold to which club in August 2021?
Al-Hilal

19) Who signed from Crystal Palace in September 2022?
Martin Kelly

20) Josh Maja signed from which club ahead of the 2023/24 season?
Bordeaux

If you enjoyed this book please consider leaving a five star review on Amazon

Books by Jack Pearson available on Amazon:

Cricket:

The Quiz Book of the England Cricket Team in the 21st Century
Cricket World Cup 2019 Quiz Book
The Ashes 2019 Cricket Quiz Book
The Ashes 2010-2019 Quiz Book
The Ashes 2005 Quiz Book
The Indian Premier League Quiz Book

Football:

The Quiz Book of Premier League Football Transfers
The Quiz Book of the England Football Team in the 21st Century
The Quiz Book of Arsenal Football Club in the 21st Century
The Quiz Book of Aston Villa Football Club in the 21st Century
The Quiz Book of Chelsea Football Club in the 21st Century

The Quiz Book of Everton Football Club in the 21st Century

The Quiz Book of Leeds United Football Club in the 21st Century

The Quiz Book of Leicester City Football Club in the 21st Century

The Quiz Book of Liverpool Football Club in the 21st Century

The Quiz Book of Manchester City Football Club in the 21st Century

The Quiz Book of Manchester United Football Club in the 21st Century

The Quiz Book of Newcastle United Football Club in the 21st Century

The Quiz Book of Southampton Football Club in the 21st Century

The Quiz Book of Sunderland Association Football Club in the 21st Century

The Quiz Book of Tottenham Hotspur Football Club in the 21st Century

The Quiz Book of West Ham United Football Club in the 21st Century

The Quiz Book of Wrexham Association Football Club in the 21st Century

Printed in Great Britain
by Amazon

30372508R00037